Purchased with Title 1 Funds
Guilford County Schools

Spain Explores the Americas

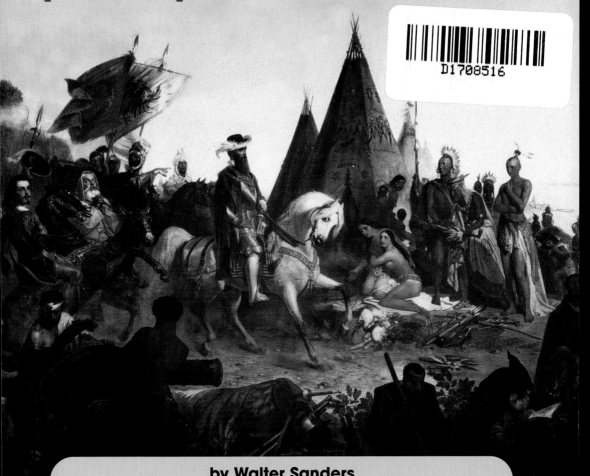

D1708516

by Walter Sanders

Table of Contents

ESL Guilford
Southeastern Region
Guilford County Schools
Greensboro, NC

T1777

Introduction

Spain explored the Americas.
Who were the **explorers** for Spain?
What did they find?

Read to learn about the explorers.

▲ Spain explored the Americas.

Words to Know

Christopher Columbus

Hernando de Cortéz

explored

explorers

Francisco Pizarro

Juan Ponce de León

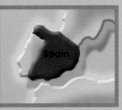

Spain

3

See the Glossary on page 22.

Who Was Christopher Columbus?

Christopher Columbus was an explorer. Columbus was an explorer for Spain. Columbus was the first explorer for Spain.

▲ Christopher Columbus was an explorer for Spain.

Columbus had three ships. Columbus went on a voyage in 1492. Columbus wanted to go to Asia.

▲ Columbus sailed from Spain.

▲ Columbus had three ships.

The ships sailed to a new place. Columbus named the place San Salvador.

Native people lived in the new place.

It's a Fact

Columbus thought the new place was in Asia. The new place was not in Asia. The new place was in North America.

▲ Columbus met native people.

Columbus went back to Spain. Columbus told about the new place. Other people wanted to go there.

▲ King Ferdinand and Queen Isabella helped Columbus.

People to Know

King Ferdinand was king of Spain. Queen Isabella was queen of Spain. Ferdinand and Isabella gave Columbus his ships.

Who Was
Juan Ponce de León?

Juan Ponce de León was an explorer.
Ponce de León was an explorer for Spain.

▲ Juan Ponce de León was an explorer for Spain.

Ponce de León went on a voyage. Ponce de León explored an island. Ponce de León explored Puerto Rico. Ponce de León wanted to find gold.

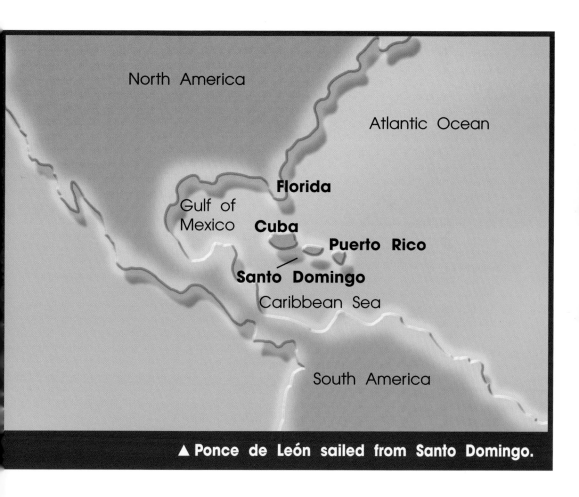

North America

Atlantic Ocean

Florida

Gulf of Mexico **Cuba**

Puerto Rico

Santo Domingo

Caribbean Sea

South America

▲ **Ponce de León sailed from Santo Domingo.**

Native people lived in Puerto Rico.

▲ The native people were the Taino.

Ponce de León fought the native people.
He became the leader of Puerto Rico.

▲ Ponce de León became leader.

11

Ponce de León went on another voyage. He explored a new land. He named the land Florida.

Did You Know?

Ponce de León looked for a Fountain of Youth. He wanted to drink the water. He wanted to be young again.

▲ Ponce de León explored Florida.

Native people lived in Florida. Ponce de León fought the native people. The native people killed Ponce de León.

▲ Ponce de León died.

13

Who Were Hernando de Cortéz and Francisco Pizarro?

Hernando de Cortéz was an explorer. Cortéz was an explorer for Spain.

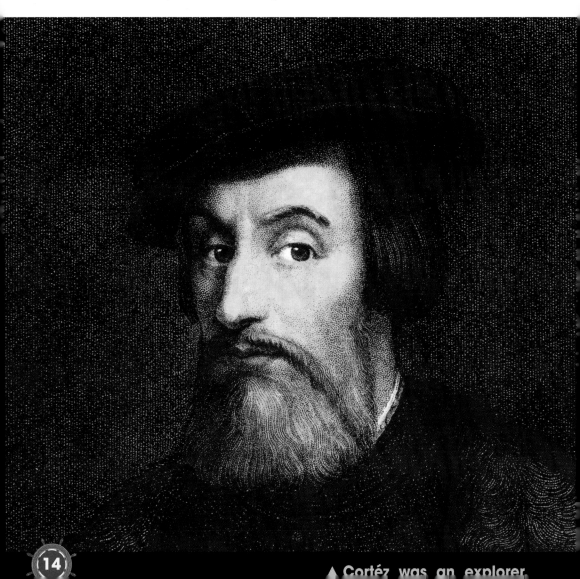

▲ Cortéz was an explorer.

Cortéz sailed to Mexico in 1519. Cortéz wanted to find gold.

Native people lived in Mexico. The native people had gold.

◀ The Aztec had gold.

North America

GULF OF MEXICO

Cuba

Tenochtitlán   Veracruz

Aztec Empire

CARIBBEAN SEA

Central America

PACIFIC OCEAN

N
W   E
S

SCALE OF MILES
0   200   400

▲ Cortéz sailed from Cuba.

▲ The native people were the Aztec.

Cortéz fought the native people.
Cortéz became the leader of Mexico.

▲ Cortéz and his men fought the Aztec.

Francisco Pizarro was an explorer. Pizarro was an explorer for Spain.

▲ Pizarro was an explorer.

It's a Fact

The explorers were conquistadors.

Francisco Pizarro sailed to Peru about 1530. Pizarro wanted to find gold.

Native people lived in Peru. The native people had gold.

▲ The native people were the Inca.

The Inca had gold. ▶

Pizarro fought the native people. Pizarro became the leader of Peru.

▲ Pizarro was the leader.

Solve This

Explorers for Spain

Explorers	When They Lived
Christopher Columbus	1451–1506
Juan Ponce de León	1460–1521
Hernando de Cortéz	1485–1547
Francisco Pizarro	1476–1541

Look at the chart. Which explorer lived the longest? How many years did he live?

Answer: Pizarro, 65 years

Summary

Spain had many explorers. The explorers wanted to find gold. The explorers fought with the natives.

first explorer for Spain
three ships
San Salvador
native people

Christopher Columbus

Spain Explores the Americas

explorer for Spain
Puerto Rico
native people
Florida
killed in Florida

Juan Ponce de León

Hernando de Cortéz

explorer for Spain
Mexico
native people
leader of Mexico

North America
Asia
Spain
Europe
Atlantic Ocean
Africa
Pacific Ocean
South America
Indian Ocean
Australia

Francisco Pizarro

explorer for Spain
Peru
native people
leader of Peru

Think About It

1. What did the explorers from Spain find?
2. Native people met explorers from Spain. What did the native people do?

Glossary

Christopher Columbus
the first explorer for Spain

*Christopher Columbus
had three ships.*

Hernando de Cortéz an
explorer for Spain

*Hernando de Cortéz
explored Mexico.*

explored went to
new places

*Christopher Columbus
explored the Americas.*

explorers people who
travel to new places

*Christopher Columbus was
an **explorer**.*

Francisco Pizarro an explorer for Spain

Francisco Pizarro explored Peru.

Juan Ponce de León an explorer for Spain

Juan Ponce de León explored Puerto Rico and Florida.

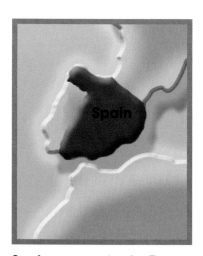

Spain a country in Europe

*Explorers came to the Americas from **Spain**.*

Purchased with Title I Funds
Guilford County Schools

Index

ESL Guilford
Southeastern Region
Guilford County Schools
Greensboro, NC

24

T 177?